W9-CEE-447

MIGHTY MACHINES

Garbage Trucks

by Mary Lindeen

BELLWETHER MEDIA • MINNEAPOLIS, MN

BLASTOFF! READERS

Note to Librarians, Teachers, and Parents:

Blastoff! Readers are carefully developed by literacy experts and combine standards-based content with developmentally-appropriate text.

Level 1 provides the most support through repetition of high-frequency words, light text, predictable sentence patterns, and strong visual support.

Level 2 offers early readers a bit more challenge through varied simple sentences, increased text load, and less repetition of high frequency words.

Level 3 advances early-fluent readers toward fluency through increased text and concept load, less reliance on visuals, longer sentences, and more literary language.

Level 4 builds reading stamina by providing more text per page, increased use of punctuation, greater variation in sentence patterns, and increasingly challenging vocabulary.

Level 5 encourages children to move from "learning to read" to "reading to learn" by providing even more text, varied writing styles, and less familiar topics.

Whichever book is right for your reader, Blastoff! Readers are the perfect books to build confidence and encourage a love of reading that will last a lifetime!

This edition first published in 2008 by Bellwether Media.

Library of Congress Cataloging-in-Publication Data
Lindeen, Mary.
  Garbage trucks / by Mary Lindeen.
    p. cm. – (Mighty machines) (Blastoff! readers)
Summary: "Simple text and supportive full-color photographs introduce young readers to garbage trucks. Intended for kindergarten through third grade students"–Provided by publisher.
  Includes bibliographical references and index.
  ISBN-13: 978-1-60014-117-1 (hardcover : alk. paper)
  ISBN-10: 1-60014-117-X (hardcover : alk. paper)
  1. Refuse collection vehicles–Juvenile literature. 2. Refuse and refuse disposal–Juvenile literature. I. Title.

TD792.L56 2008
629.225–dc22

Contents

A **garbage** truck is a big machine. It carries smelly **cargo**!

Workers empty garbage cans into garbage trucks.

A **packer blade** packs garbage down. This makes space for more.

packer blade

This **front-loading** garbage truck has an arm.

arm

The arm lifts a metal **bin** over the cab. It empties it into the truck.

arm

An **automated** garbage truck lifts garbage cans from the side.

Some garbage trucks use a **bucket** to pick up very heavy garbage.

bucket

Garbage trucks unload at **landfills**.

Now it's time
to go pick up
more garbage!

Glossary

automated—the use of machines rather than people to do jobs

bin—a large metal box that holds trash

bucket—a part of a machine that is used for lifting, scooping, or carrying heavy objects

cargo—a load carried by a truck, ship, plane, or train

front-loading—to load from the front

garbage—things that are thrown away

landfill—a place where garbage is dumped and buried under layers of dirt

packer blade— the broad, flat part inside a garbage truck; the packer blade pushes down the garbage to make it smaller.

To Learn More

AT THE LIBRARY

Alinas, Marv. *Garbage Trucks*. Mankato, Minn.: Child's Worlds, 2007.

Bridges, Sarah. *I Drive a Garbage Truck*. Mankato, Minn.: Picture Window Books, 2006.

Brill, Marlene Targ. *Garbage Trucks*. Minneapolis, Minn.: Lerner, 2004.

Clark, Katie. *Grandma Drove the Garbage Truck*. Camden, Maine: Down East Books, 2006.

ON THE WEB

Learning more about mighty machines is as easy as 1, 2, 3.

1. Go to www.factsurfer.com

2. Enter "mighty machines" into search box.

3. Click the "Surf" button and you will see a list of related web sites.

With factsurfer.com, finding more information is just a click away.

Index

The photographs in this book are reproduced through the courtesy of: McNeilus, front cover; pp. 5, 7, 9, 11, 13, 15, 17, 21; Jeff Smith/Alamy, p. 19.